TECH SMARTS

12 QUESTIONS ABOUT SOCIAL MEDIA

BLACK RABBIT BOOKS

MARNE VENTURA

Table of Contents

There are a variety of ways for people to share information by text.

What Is *Social Media?*

1

Before the internet, people read newspapers and magazines. They listened to the radio. They watched TV. This is how they got news. They could talk about what they learned. But they could only do this in person. Today, people can react in real-time to breaking news. The internet makes it possible. People use social media to talk to each other **online**.

Social media is a platform to share information. You can reach a large audience. Social media uses websites and apps. Popular sites include Facebook, X (formerly Twitter), TikTok, YouTube, and Pinterest. People post and share **visual** media. They share videos and pictures. Unlike an email, this information is public. It can be seen by many others. This includes family, friends, and sometimes strangers. You may never

Many people have turned to social media for their news instead of newspapers.

know who has seen your posts. You may see posts from people you don't know.

Social **networks** are a form of social media. They focus on communication and building relationships. Snapchat and Instagram are social networks. Many social media sites, like Facebook, are also networks. These sites are like giant cities. Your family and friends are your neighborhood. You can connect with them to talk. You can share photos and links. Networking helps you keep in touch with your digital neighbors.

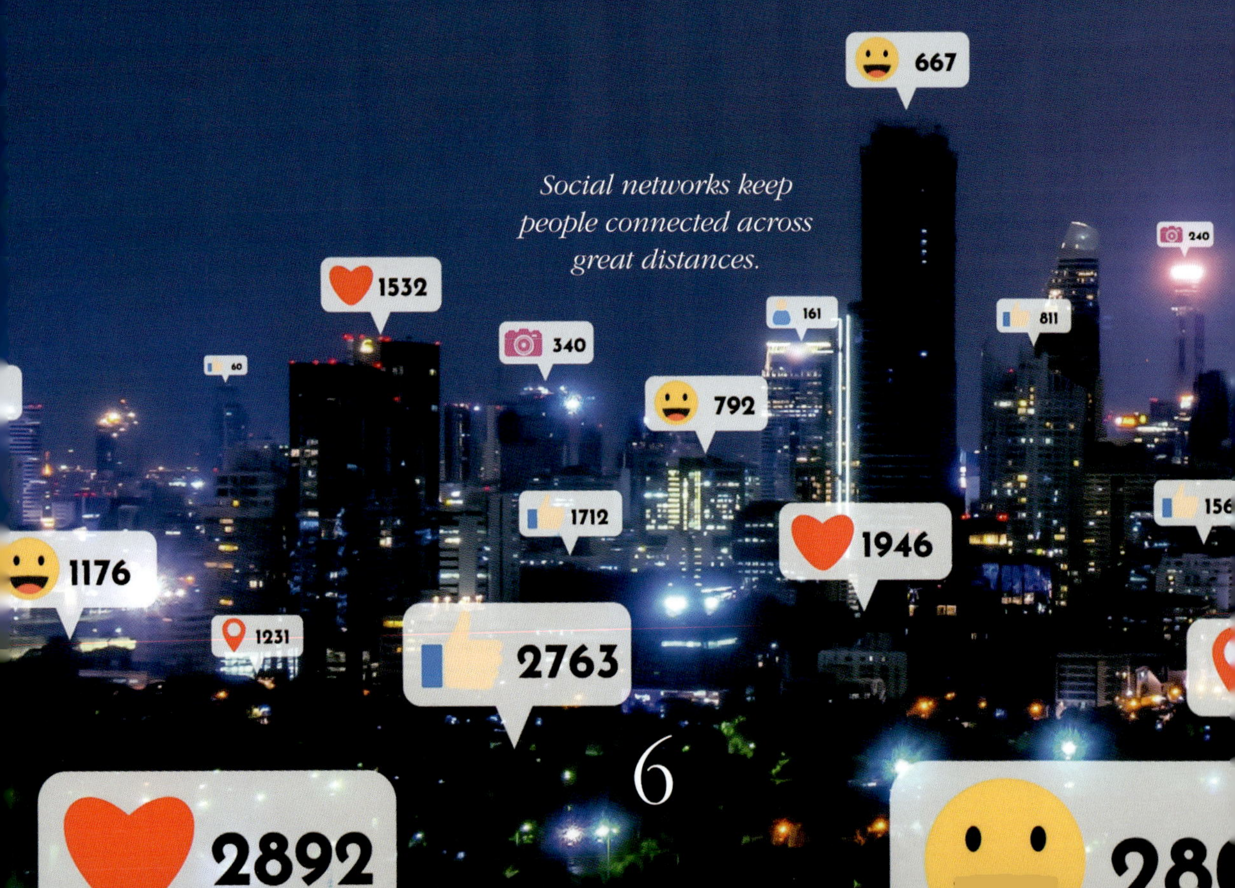

Social networks keep people connected across great distances.

71 Percent of US teens who visited YouTube daily in 2023.

TikTok users were the second largest group at 58 percent. • The third largest group was Snapchat users at 51 percent. • Instagram was fourth largest at 47 percent.

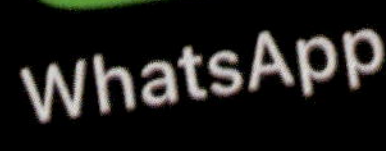

Social media apps help people stay in-touch from anywhere.

What Can I Do on *Social Media?*

2

Social media helps you talk to friends. It can also be fun. Use social networks to send news to friends. Ask a friend to play checkers. Share photos of your art project. Make short videos and post them. You can even work with classmates on school projects.

Sharing things on social media is easy. Finding the right social media site can be harder. The most well-known sites are Facebook, X, and Instagram. These are for teens and adults. Kids younger than 13 are not allowed to join.

There are sites just for kids, like Messenger Kids. It is the under-13 messaging app where you can send text chats and pictures to approved friends. There are many more kids social media sites. Share short videos on Zigazoo. Chat with friends and share posts on

20 Percentage of 9 to 12-year-olds who use social media every day.

Social media lets users share their interests with friends. • Kids can learn about different places and ways of thinking. • Kids with disabilities or who live far away can connect with others online.

Some social media sites let you make video calls.

Grom Social. Make video calls on Kinzoo Messenger. Play games at Azoomee. Connect with your family on GeckoLife. Make your own **virtual** world on PK XD. Watch silly videos on YouTube Kids. All these sites are a good way to get started with social media. They are made with kids' privacy and safety in mind. They are also made for fun.

Messenger Kids has extra safety features and does not require a phone number.

Is Social Media *Free?*

3

Most social networks are free to use. There is no sign-up fee for X, Facebook, or Instagram. You can make comments, post photos, and read news for free. But users will still see ads. This is how the sites make money. Most kids' sites are also free. They usually don't have as many ads. Sites like Kidzworld let you read news and take fun quizzes for free.

Ads lets social media sites give their services to users for free. Advertisers pay to run their ads on social media sites. They may pay extra to make sure more people will see the ad. Advertisers can even focus on a specific group of users. They may only want to show the ad to teens or new parents. Social media sites have this data. They track it in their own sites. Advertisers pay social media sites to target these audiences with their ads. When you click on an ad, advertisers make money. They may benefit from you buying their product as well.

Sometimes it's a quick post you can easily scroll past. Other times it's a video that you might not realize is an ad at first. Ads don't cost you money. But they may cost your time and attention. YouTube started running ads in videos in 2007. At first, they were transparent and skippable. Today, there are longer ads that you may not be able to skip. Longer videos even have ads in the middle.

THINK ABOUT IT

Social media influencers are often paid to promote products. This is a form of advertisement. How might this affect a user differently than a regular ad?

$234 billion Estimated amount of money spent on social media ads in 2024 worldwide.

This number is expected to grow by 50 percent by 2029. • Facebook and Instagram run the most ads. • Short-form videos are the biggest social media trend.

Brands pay influencers to promote their products.

How Do Social Networks Benefit *from Users?*

4

Social networks are businesses. Their goal is to make money. They do this by selling ads. The price of an ad is based on how many people view it. The more users they have, the better chance that the ad will sell products. When advertisers sell products, they place more ads. This means the site makes more money.

Social networks keep track of their users. They know their age and gender. They know where they live. They know what they like and do not like. They learn this by tracking which content they click on. A user who likes to bake may watch videos about baking. The site remembers this. It shares more baking content with the user. It will also post ads for baking supplies and tools. This makes the user want to return to the site. The site hopes the user will buy the products in the ads.

Before the internet, people saw video ads in the movie theater and on TV.

Social networks learn to post things that will interest you. This can be fun. It can help you learn more about your interests. But it is important to be aware. You don't want social media to limit the information you get.

Targeted ads are common on social media.

Is Social Media *Safe?*

5

It is hard to know whom you can trust online. People are not always honest. They might hide who they are. To be safe, limit your online friends. Only talk to people you know in real life.

Social media can be a safe and fun place. But you should follow some guidelines. Remember that what you post is public. Friends and family can see it. Some strangers may even find it. Do not share your address, birthday, or phone number. The same goes for your school name. This is private information. You want to keep this safe. Do not post your Social Security or bank numbers. This is **confidential** information. In the wrong hands, it could cause you a lot of harm. These things can be used by strangers. They might know how to find you. They might pretend to be you, which is called identity theft. Instead, share your interests. Post about activities you like.

Closely guard your passwords. Only you and your parents should know the login information. This stops other people from getting your private information. And they won't be able to pretend to be you online. Kids can stay safe on social media. It is all about smart decisions. If information is personal, keep it private.

40 Percentage of US children ages 8 to 12 who use social media.

Don't post your location. • Learn how to use privacy settings. • Don't "friend" or answer posts from strangers.

Each post, follow, like,
and comment builds
your online identity.

TAG, YOU'RE HERE!

It is best to not post your location in real time. But even if you don't, your social network might! This is called geo-tagging. A network can include your location on a post. You can stop this. It is part of your settings. Ask an adult how to turn this off. Do this on all accounts and devices.

Should I Share My Accounts with *My Parents?*

6

Learning to be safe online takes practice. This is true even for kids' sites. For most sites, you need a parent to sign up. Then both you and your parent can log in. The parent can help you stay safe.

Kids' websites have extra protections. A **federal** law keeps this in check. It is the Children's Online Privacy Protection Act (COPPA). The law protects users younger than 13. It puts parents in control to decide what information gets shared. A kid needs a parent's or guardian's permission to sign up. Most sites require your name and an email. Some collect phone numbers, locations, and usernames. Kids' sites must protect this information. They can store it, but it cannot be **accessible**. And the site cannot share it without the parent's permission.

If you are younger than 13, ask your parents for help. They can sign you up on a kids-only social media site. Ask them to share their social media sites with you. Look at family photos on Instagram. Browse their social networks with them. Ask questions. Together, you can learn about social media. You can decide what rules work for your family.

Parental controls keep kids safe from harmful sites and people.

A child's personal information is more secure on kid-friendly sites.

61 Percent of parents who monitor their children's social networking activity.

TikTok, Instagram, and Snapchat have parental control settings. • Parents can monitor and turn off certain videos or comments. • This helps parents make sure you are using social media safely.

Should I Express My Feelings on *Social Media?*

7

People often journal to feel better. They write down things that happened and how they are feeling. It gives them a chance to think things through. Social media is not journaling. Other users can see what you write or share. You can tear up a piece of paper. But posts online stay there forever. You can delete a message or post. But a backup might exist. And you can't control how other people use your post. They may share it on their account. They might save your message or take a screenshot. Your name will be linked to it forever.

It is easy to be brave behind a computer screen. People are more likely to say mean things online than they are in real life. Do not post hurtful things. You might make someone else feel bad. You also make yourself look bad. Information you share on social media never really goes away. Future friends, colleges, and even bosses

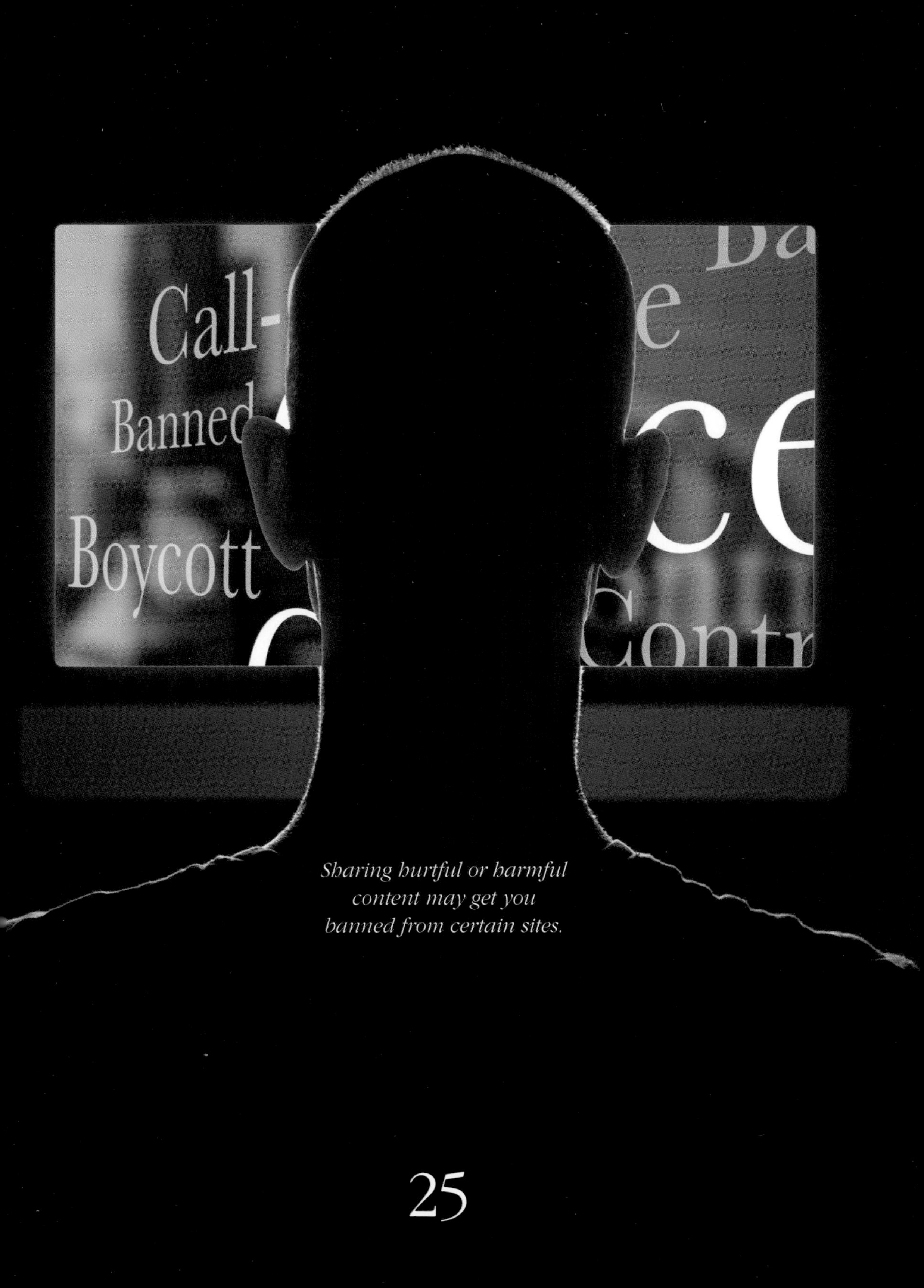

Sharing hurtful or harmful content may get you banned from certain sites.

may find it years later. Don't share gossip or unkind posts. Don't use bad language. Before posting, ask yourself, "Would I want my grandma to see this?" If the answer is no, then do not post it.

A HISTORY IN TWEETS

In 2010, the Library of Congress started a new collection. It saved all public tweets from X. The archive goes back to 2006. It was a big job. More than 500 million tweets are sent by Americans every day. The archive is like an oral history of the social media era. Starting in 2018, the Library now only saves select tweets.

What Should I Post on *Social Media?*

8

When you share something on social media, a lot of people see it. It makes sense to be careful about what you post. Social media is a good place to share about positive things. People often update followers on big life events. They post about birthdays and graduations. They share fun moments, like concerts and trips.

You can share what you enjoy online. Post about your interests. Did you read a good book? Tell others, so they can enjoy it. Did your sports team win? Are you learning to paint or sew? Post good news. Share information that will be fun or helpful to others. Be sure the information is true and correct.

When you comment on someone else's posts, be kind. You can use social media to thank or recognize someone else. Nice messages on social media are powerful. It feels good to make someone smile. Kindness can be

45 million Number of pictures posted on Instagram every day.

Share poems, funny videos, or ask good questions. • Post photos of field trips or fun STEM activities. • Ask friends which movies or TV shows they like. • Always ask permission before posting photos or videos of others.

Some people share beautiful pictures they took on social media.

contagious, too. Others will share your comments. They might be inspired to post their own.

Social media is not limited to words. You can also share pictures. Post photos of your latest artwork or a family party. Before you post, ask. Make sure everyone in the picture is okay with your posting it. Some people don't want their faces or names on the internet.

What If Someone Bothers Me on *Social Media?*

9

Some people do not follow the rules of social media. They share untrue or unkind things about other people. These people are called cyberbullies.

There are ways to deal with an online bully. First, do not reply to their posts. Write down the times and dates of when you were bullied. Print out a copy. Take a picture of the post. You can report the bully to the social media site. The bully might use a fake name. But the company might be able to learn who they are. The company may ban them from using the site. If the bully is from your school, report them to the principal. Some posts might make you afraid or uneasy. If this is the case, ask an adult for help. Report the bully to the police.

There is no federal law that bans cyberbullying. But it is against the law in almost all states. How schools deal with bullies varies from state to state. In some states, schools can expel or suspend them. In other states, schools can call on police for help.

A cyberbully might send cruel messages directly to their target.

THINK ABOUT IT

Imagine that your friend is being cyberbullied. What advice would you give them?

Cyberbullying can feel very isolating to victims.

1 in 3 Number of middle and high school students who have been bullied online.
Only 40 percent of online bullying victims report it to their parents. • Only 30 percent of victims report it to a teacher. • Social media is the number one cyberbullying platform.

Can Social Media *Help Me Learn?*

10 Social media has changed the way people **converse**. You can post your thoughts as soon as you have them. People can **collaborate** more easily. They can share facts and ideas anytime. This is helpful for learning. Scientists and news outlets may post about their latest findings. Many kids' learning sites have a Facebook page. You can find interesting facts on National Geographic Kids. You can comment on the sites. You can share them with your friends.

Social media helps students work together. You can plan a project with friends on social media. You can share ideas. You can post articles and pictures. Connect with classmates by video chat. Some teachers list class work on a **blog**. Students can post comments. One teacher in Brooklyn, New York, uses X to share resources and tips for studying. Schools can send tweets or texts about

Some teachers record their lessons and post them online for students.

88 Percent of parents who think YouTube helps their child learn new things.

Social media can be a great tool for learning. • Kids can find videos on how to cook, make crafts, or play an instrument. • They can also find answers to questions they have about their interests.

upcoming events. You can check your school's social media pages for updates on events.

Some social media sites are just for schools. Google Classroom is a free site for schools. Teachers create, post, and grade work. Students take quizzes and submit work online. Teachers give feedback on student work. They can both share files online. Thanks to social media, the classroom never closes. Lessons can keep going even after the final bell rings.

Many schools hav
e-learning days wher
students learn onlin

How Can I Use Social Media *to Connect?*

11

Social media can connect you with faraway friends. Maybe you have a cousin in a different state. You only see them once or twice a year. With social media, you can stay in touch more often. Social media also helps you connect with friends at home. Maybe you are working on a report with classmates. Sometimes you can't meet at the library or school. But you can still meet up on social media. You can share notes and ideas at any time online.

Social media is a way to help out in your community. Do you think recycling is important? You can share posts with ideas on how to reuse items. Is your church or scout troop trying to raise money for a good cause? Post about it on social media. Do you and your friends want to start a community garden at your school? Let others know about it with social media. You can sell and donate items online. You can also look for community events.

Social media lets you learn about people around the world. You might not be able to travel to Asia. But you can see pictures of it online. You can read about what kids your age do for fun.

7 million Pounds (3.2 million kg) of food given to families in need by Joshua's Heart Foundation.

When Joshua was 4, he asked his family to help him fight hunger. • They used social media to ask for volunteers and money. • Many of the volunteers are young people.

Women build a roof for a home for Habitat for Humanity in Oakland, California.

HELPING BUILD HOMES Habitat for Humanity builds homes for people in need. J.Z. was a 10-year-old boy in Texas. He asked for donations instead of gifts for his birthday. He raised $70 for Habitat for Humanity. They posted his donation on social media. Other people were inspired to give more money.

Do I Need to Be on *Social Media?*

12 Social media is not a basic need. Basic needs are things you need to stay alive. Food, water, and shelter are basic needs. Social media is one way to connect with friends. You can keep in touch with family and friends in many ways. You can call or text them. You can meet up in person.

People spend hours a day on social media. This is often more time than they spend with friends in real life. Research shows that too much time on social media can be harmful. In 2024, a study found that using social media causes some kids to be **anxious**. It makes some kids feel that they are not good enough.

If you use social media, set limits for yourself. Log in just once or twice a day. Do not compare yourself to others on social media. Remember, most people use social media to show themselves at their best. Their lives might look perfect. But they have problems and worries just like you. Social media is like any other hobby. Use it if you enjoy it. If it stops being fun, do something else.

SCREEN TIME

American children ages 8 to 12 average 4 to 6 hours per day watching or using screens. Experts say 1 to 2 hours per day is a healthy limit. Too much screen time can cause problems with sleep. It can take the place of healthy exercise.

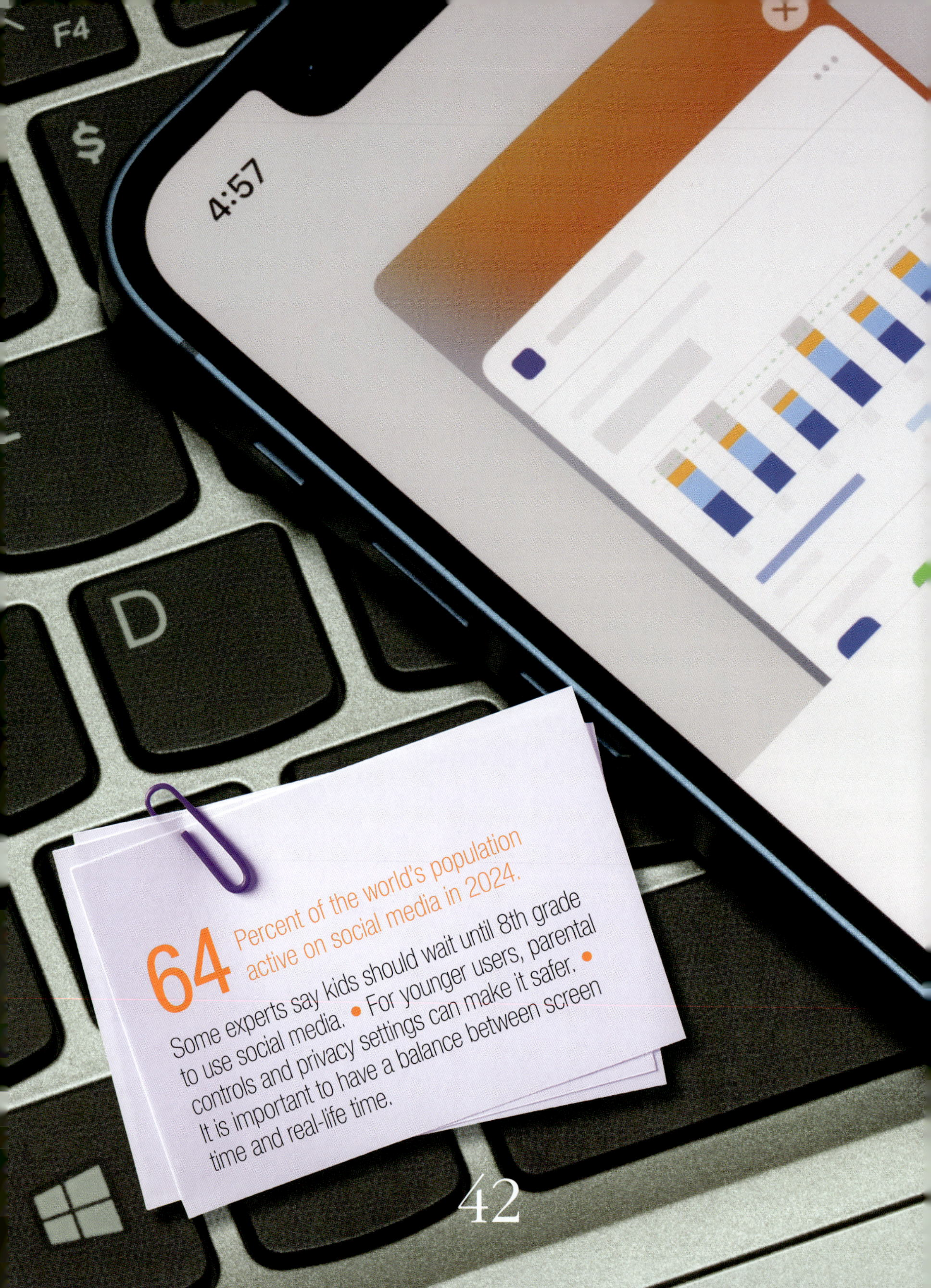

64 Percent of the world's population active on social media in 2024.

Some experts say kids should wait until 8th grade to use social media. • For younger users, parental controls and privacy settings can make it safer. • It is important to have a balance between screen time and real-life time.

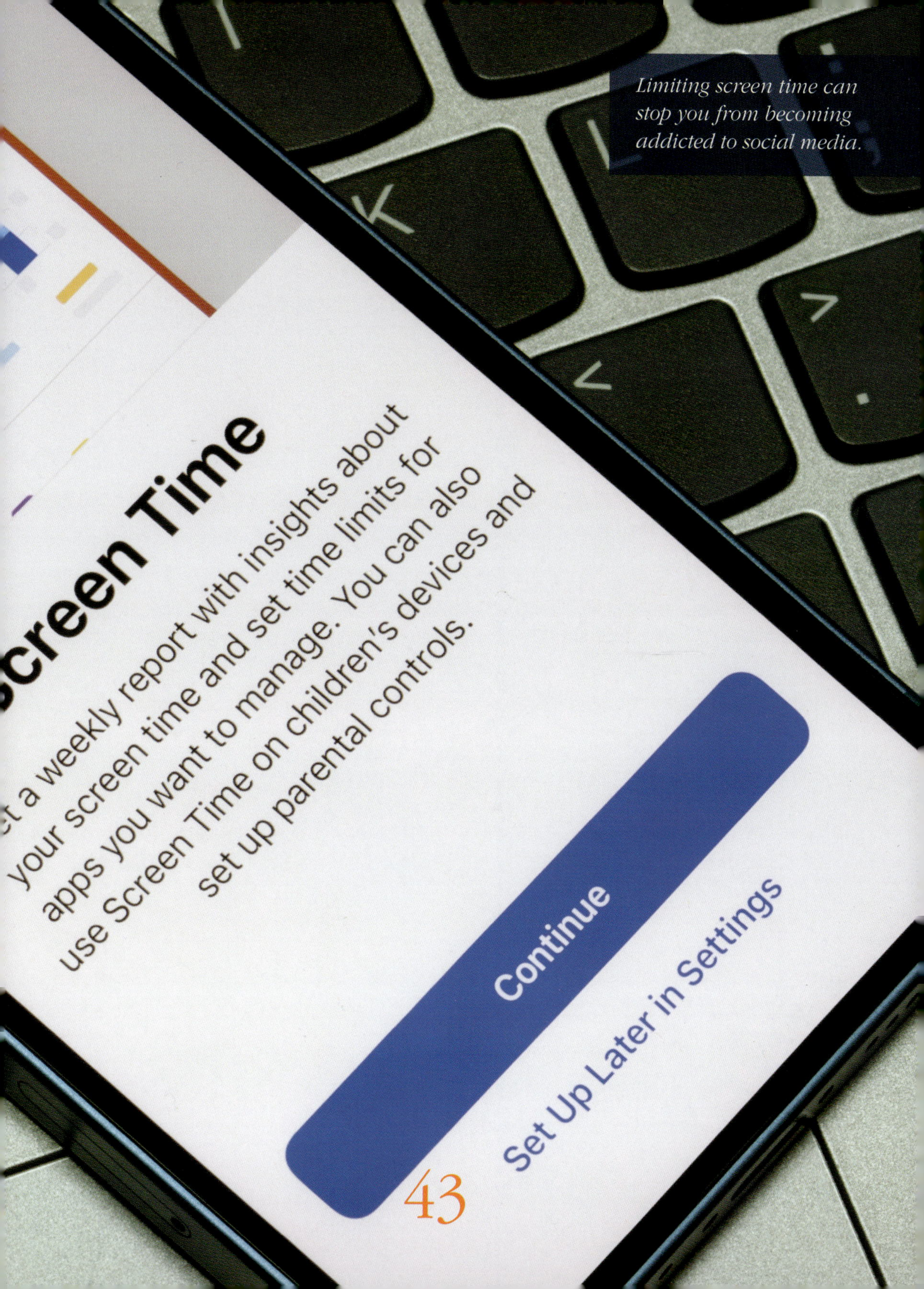

Limiting screen time can stop you from becoming addicted to social media.

Safety Tips for

Find the Right Social Media

Do some research on each platform or network. It's fun to join a site that your friends are all on. But there may be a different site that is more aligned to your interests. Users must be at least 13 years old for Facebook, TikTok, or Instagram. But there are plenty of sites designed for younger users. Create an account on a site that's made for your age group.

Limit Your Online Friends

Do not "friend" anyone you don't know in real life. Use your social media account to connect with classmates. Reach out to cousins or grandparents who live far away. Do not accept friend requests from strangers.

Social Media

Keep Information Private

Your real name, address, and birth date should be private. Don't share them online. Don't post photos that show where you live or go to school. Predators may use this information to find you. Don't post the dates when your family will be gone on vacation. Criminals could use this to rob you.

Share with Your Parents

Share your passwords and usernames with your parents. They can make sure you are staying safe online. Even when you're careful, strangers or cyberbullies can find you. Your parents can help you learn how to stay safe. They can teach you the benefits of social media without the problems.

Glossary

accessible
Able to be used or obtained.

anxious
Afraid or nervous, especially about what may happen.

blog
A website on which someone writes about personal opinions, activities, and experiences.

collaborate
To work with another person or group in order to achieve or do something.

confidential
Secret or private.

converse
To talk informally with someone.

federal
Of or relating to the national government.

network
A system of computers or other devices that are connected to each other.

online
Connected to a computer, network, or the internet.

virtual
Happening online.

visual
Relating to seeing or to the eyes.

For More Information

Books

Green, Sara. *TikTok*. Minneapolis: Bellwether Media, Inc., 2024.

Kallen, Stuart A. *The Power of Social Media*. San Diego: ReferencePoint Press, 2024.

Mann, Dionna L. *The Genius of Facebook: How Mark Zuckerburg and Social Media Changed the World*. Minneapolis: Lerner Publications, 2023.

Peters, Jackson. *Instagram: The Story Behind the App*. Hollywood, FL: Mason Crest, 2024.

Websites

Internet Safety Course
edu.gcfglobal.org/en/internetsafety/

Social Media
kids.britannica.com/students/article/social-media/635756

Social Media Tips for Kids and Teens
health.choc.org/handout/social-media-tips-for-kids-and-teens/

About the Author

Marne Ventura is the author of more than 150 books for children. A former elementary school teacher, she holds a master's degree in reading and language development from the University of California. Ventura and her family live in California.

Index

TOP RANK is published by Black Rabbit Books, P.O. Box 227, Mankato, MN, 56002. • Designed by Danny Nanos • Photographs © Alamy Stock Photo/Pictorial Press, 14–15; Dreamstime/Andrew Angelov, 9, Cammeraydave, 32–33, Dmytro Zinkevych, 38, Prostockstudio, 31, Vladislav Kochelaevskiy, 23; Shutterstock/ Belinda Pretorius, 48, Billion Photos, 41, chainarong06, 20, Chay_Tee, 2, 11, 13, Eric Isselee, 12, Fabio Principe, 21, Ground Picture, 34, IfH, cover, 1, ISARA SUKSARN, 38, Jakub Krechowicz, 2–3, 4–5, Javidestock, 22, jittawit21, 12, Jolygon, 46–47, KOTOIMAGES, 27, Linaimages, 45, Mariusz S. Jurgielewicz, 37, MindStorm, 39, Natasha Breen, 16, New Africa, 12, one photo, 45, PeopleImages.com - Yuri A, 25, Primakov, 7, Roman Samborskyi, 44, Sander van der Werf, 24, 25, sansandra, 16, sdx15, 10, SewCreamStudio, 41, sitthiphong, 8, ssi77, 26, Summit Art Creations, 6, Tada Images, 42–43, 44, tanuha2001, 5, TSViPhoto, 18–19, TZIDO SUN, 35, Ulza, 36, ymgerman, 22 • Printed in India

Library of Congress Cataloging-in-Publication Data: Names: Ventura, Marne, author. | Title: 12 questions about social media / by Marne Ventura. | Other titles: Twelve questions about social media | Description: Mankato, MN: Top Rank, an imprint of Black Rabbit Books, [2026] | Series: Tech smarts | Includes bibliographical references and index. | Ages 9–13 | Grades 4–6 | Identifiers: LCCN 2024054686 (print) | LCCN 2024054687 (ebook) | ISBN 9781644668191 (library binding) | ISBN 9781644668511 (paperback) | ISBN 9781644668832 (ebook) | Subjects: LCSH: Social media—Juvenile literature. | Online social networks—Juvenile literature. | Internet and children—Juvenile literature. | Internet and teenagers—Juvenile literature. | Internet—Safety measures—Juvenile literature. | Classification: LCC HM742 .V46 2026 (print) | LCC HM742 (ebook) | DDC 302.23/1—dc23/eng/20241210 | LC record available at https://lccn.loc.gov/2024054686